Francis Lewis Gould

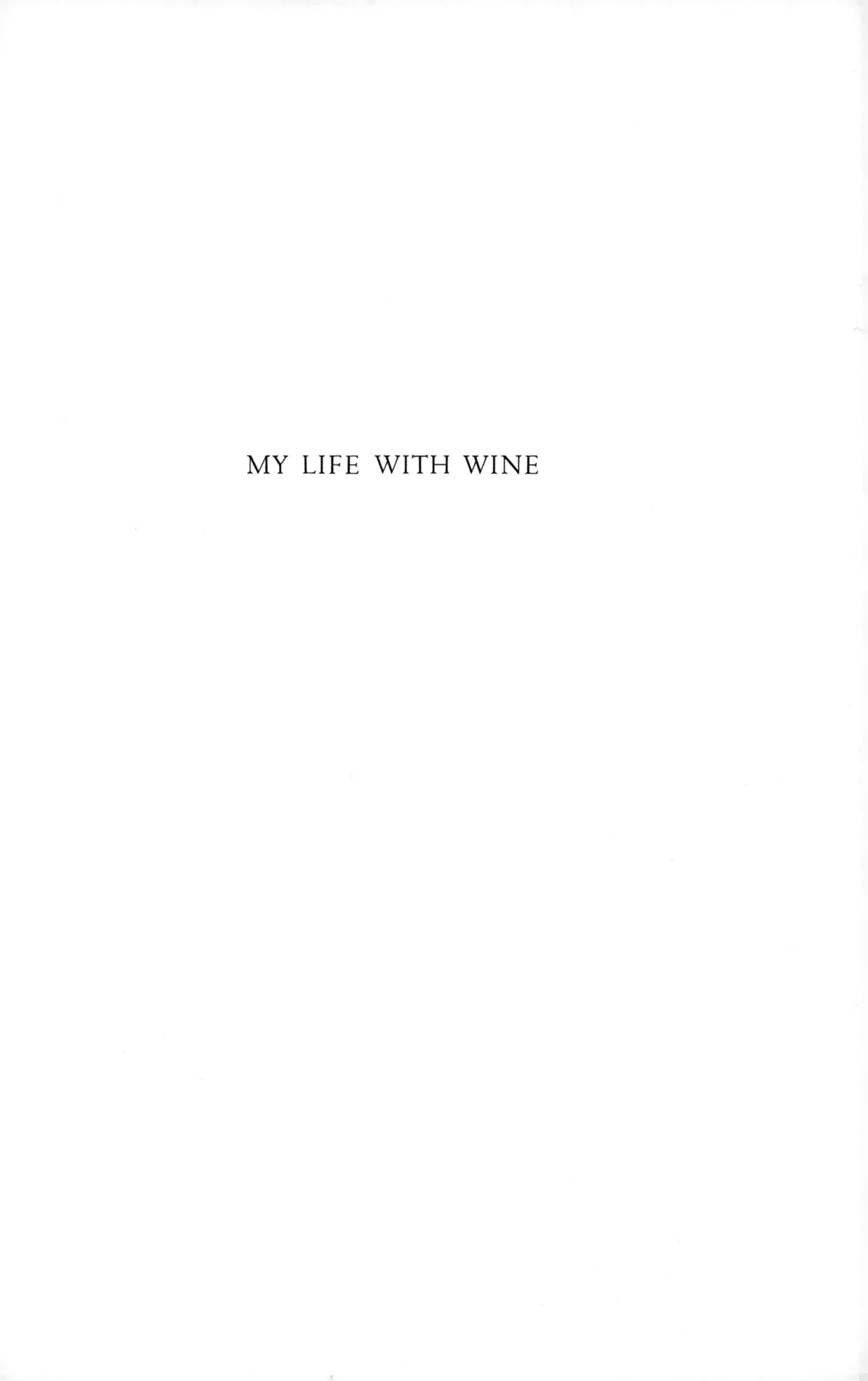

MY LIFE WITH WINE

Portrait by Taylor Biggs Lewis

FRANCIS LEWIS GOULD

MY LIFE WITH WINE

ST. HELENA, CALIFORNIA :: 1972

Printed in the United States of America

Dedicated to the
Readers of
"Bottles and Bins"

CONTENTS

INTRODUCTION

IT IS DIFFICULT *and perhaps impossible to write an introduction for this little book without becoming personal, for anyone who knows Francis Lewis Gould.*

In my own case, I have been his friend for twenty-five years (not long enough!), and I cannot help comparing him with three other 'sons of Bacchus' whom I also admire: Brillat-Savarin, Sam Ward, and André Simon. Together, they make an impressive quartet, and singly each of them deserves respect as well as affection. They share the same sharp yet benevolent view of their fellowmen.

Chronologically Brillat-Savarin was born in 1755; Sam Ward, 'king of the lobby', in 1814; André Simon in 1877. Paco Gould, as close friends call him, appeared on the scene in 1884, and hence is the only member of the company I have known face to face, eye to eye, of these four men who are so astonishingly alike.

They have all lived long lives, filled with the warmth and excitement of being gusty yet discriminating males. They seem to have fed from the same fountain of youth, enjoying everything good that Life offered them, and spurning satiety of any of their five or six senses.

Brillat-Savarin died, physically at least, at the age of seventy-one, almost a phenomenon in an age when the average toll was about half that figure. He led a quietly full life, finding friends and a good meal and an excellent bottle wherever he went, from France to America and back again.

Sam Ward, another Compleat Gentleman, followed the Paris lawyer's path, whether he knew it or not, combining an honorable profession (Is politicking in Lincoln's Washington any more corrupt than being a French lawyer?) with a full-blown yet sensitive gift for enjoyment, for plain fun.

André Simon had fun too. He worked hard, and ate and drank moderately and well, and pleased everybody he met. He was a charmer of both men and women.

Paco Gould is another charmer, another literate witty wise old man. He has drunk well for some seven decades, and is equipped not only with a level head but with a superbly healthy body, so that he can digest a meal that would floor a stevedore, whether it be a bowl of good soup and a tumbler of jug-wine or a twelve-course banquet, with several choice vintage bottles.

It is interesting to me that these four men have lived such sane and lengthy lives, all the while indulging their senses in ways that would make a true Puritan fall in a faint, and yet staying courteous graceful gentlemen, never dull, never crude. They have kept themselves in good health, with all their glands clicking along like the parts of a Swiss watch, even when words like pituitary and estrogen were unknown to them and their peers. They have all been practical thinkers, in their own ways: a lawyer; a powerful politician; a founder of the worldwide Wine and Food Society and tireless author of books on the two related subjects; and now Francis Gould, who has done everything he mentions in this memoir, and a lot more, and who decided not long ago to tell about his life with wine, in case it might interest people like me. . .

Paco is the best result of a long life spent in judicious sampling of all its blessings, but especially wine, that I have met. He writes in this book that wine appeared regularly on his family table, when he was growing up. I wish that more of us could say as much. There is no better way to insure proper digestion of good food, and at the same time instill a knowledge of the wisdom of moderation, than to have young people observe and share the daily consumption of a sane amount of honest wine, whether it be vintage or jug quality.

Here again we can learn from one of our four beloved teachers! Paco invited me to dinner on his eighty-eighth birthday, and to honor his wife Romilda, and the three of us friends, he wore the black velvet dinner jacket in his little house in Northern California, that had been fitted to exactly the same measurements for his coming-of-age party in New York when he was twenty-one. (He also ate his way majestically, enthusiastically through five artful courses of a meal that I doubt could have been planned, prepared, served as well at Delmonico's, when that meant the best. What is more, he poured five bottles of high-quality wine, with delicate precision and the requisite slow savoring. . .)

This book in your hands was written about his life with wine, solely so that many more of us mortals might reach his own level of enjoyment, for Frank Gould is basically a teacher. He wants others to learn what he himself has learned. He ends his little collection of reminiscences and observations by toasting us: 'To your health, dear younger sons and daughters of Bacchus!'

As the calendars tell it, I am more a beldame than a daughter

. . . but all the true offspring of the god of wine are ageless. Paco is a sterling example of this, as were his peers of other centuries, eminently sane human beings, wearing their years with a shared jauntiness. It is comforting to believe that the rest of us have inherited some of their joie de vivre, indirectly through all of the good bottles we have learned to open and empty, and directly through reading such modest and perhaps ageless books as this.

Our four teachers have written primers for us, simple no matter how subtly worded, and they share the same debonair enjoyment, the same deathless twinkle that we can catch and perhaps make our own. We are fortunate.

M. F. K. Fisher

FOREWORD

DURING the last score of my fourscore and eight years, (may Honest Abe forgive me) many people have urged me to write a book on the wine regions of Europe and America because they knew I have had considerable acquaintance with these areas.

What they did not know is something of which I am well aware. It takes years of travel, painstaking research, countless interviews and other labors to produce a wine book that is both factual and instructive. Even when completed, the volume may need revision before publication, for the wine scene changes so rapidly that nobody can write fast enough to keep up to date.

I am too indolent to attempt such an arduous adventure. To me, wine is fun, not toil. Besides, hundreds of wine books have been written over the ages. Some, undoubtedly, are trash; but many are very good—better, I am sure, than anything I could put together. So why write just "another" wine book?

This does not mean I have been idle. For nearly forty years I have spoken and written about wine through such outlets as lectures, newspaper and magazine articles and tasting comments. In 1949 I began to write *Bottles and Bins,* the wine quarterly of Charles Krug Winery, owned and operated by C. Mondavi &

Sons, St. Helena, California. This and a cookbook called *Bottles and Bins Recipes* have been the works for which I am best known. They are the reason for this volume's dedication to the readers of *Bottles and Bins,* and the inclusion of articles from the quarterly.

I must admit that *My Life With Wine* represents a compromise. I have no stomach for the formal wine book my well wishers requested; but I have a yen to relate my experiences with wine from youth onward, including episodes that have tickled my risibilities and, I hope, will do the same for you.

It is customary for an author to mention those who have helped in the preparation of a book. I give sincere thanks to my wife, Romilda, and to M. F. K. Fisher, two ladies dear to my heart. Also, to Norman H. Strouse, Alice Riach, Lucy Brown and to one of my earliest friends in Napa Valley, James E. Beard, who has been the pilot of this little wine vessel.

FRANCIS LEWIS GOULD

St. Helena, California
May, 1972

MY LIFE WITH WINE

Who loves not wine, women and song
Remains a fool his whole life long.
—*Attributed to* MARTIN LUTHER

My love of song is real, but as a non-participant, for I cannot carry a tune. My love of women is prodigious, although I believe they are unfathomable. My love of wine is proverbial. On this score I hope I am no fool.
—F. L. G.

YOUNG AND GAY

MY INITIATION to wine drinking came at the age of six or thereabouts. It was a wishy-washy performance, as considerably more water than wine was put into my glass. Nevertheless, it was an epochal experience, because the very first sip started an affinity that has been a lifelong joy and a solace in times of stress.

I was born at White Plains, N. Y. on January 9, 1884. By arriving around midnight on that cold winter's night, thus making trouble for mother, doctor, father, et al., I gave an exhibition of my cussedness right at the start. (Don't blame me; I was born that way.)

My father was Edward Sherman Gould, my mother Arabella Duncan Ludlow (Gould), both descended from early American Colonial families. The major part of my father's scientific education was acquired at the French Military Engineering School at St. Etienne. While there, he developed a fondness for wine, and learned nearly as much about it as he did about differential calculus, a subject on which he later became an international authority. My two brothers followed his footsteps in the engineering profession. As I can't tell a slide rule from a bunghole, my father's knowledge of wine was what fascinated me. He was my mentor and was pleased to find me an avid pupil.

Shortly after my birth, we moved into an old-fashioned house above the eastern bank of the Hudson River on the outskirts of Yonkers, N. Y., built by my maternal grandfather, Edward Greenleaf Ludlow. He was a beloved practitioner of what is a nearly extinct profession—the country doctor. Like other houses of its era, ours had three stories and a large basement with cellars well suited for wine storage.

At that time our family consisted of my grandmother, Mary Kennedy Lewis Ludlow (great grand-daughter of Francis Lewis, a signer of the Declaration of Independence), my parents, my older brothers, Edward Ludlow and John Warren Du Bois, and a younger sister, Susan Mary.

My early teens, well beyond the watered-down stage, brought an increasing appreciation of wine as a beverage. There was ample opportunity to enjoy it, for wine appeared regularly on our family table. I began to take notice of what my father bought for his cellar. There were French chateau-bottlings and good German wines, and also a little Sherry and Port. He was frugal with these, reserving them mainly for discriminating guests. French regional wines were our customary fare.

One day I saw a bottle with a label strange to me. It was a California wine called "Zinfandel". Father bought a case as an experiment. What part of California it came from and which winery made it I don't remember. It might have come from Napa Valley, perhaps from the Charles Krug cellars. Anyhow, we all liked it, so Zinfandel became a regular in the bins.

During schoolboy years at the Yonkers High School, my wine drinking was largely confined to home consumption. Not many country families drank wine at the turn of the century. Coffee, tea, cocoa, milk, beer and cider were the usual beverages. However, on trips to New York City, particularly when we visited my Aunt Susan, we always indulged. She had a well-stocked wine cellar. Her husband, J. Kearny Warren, a distinguished gentleman of the old school, died when I was about twelve years old. The main thing I remember about his funeral was a startling incident that occurred at the family service before the casket was taken to Old Trinity Church for the Episcopal service and interment in the Ludlow vault. J. Pierpont Morgan, an old friend and pall bearer, banged his massive head on an equally massive chandelier; the whole room trembled, but the Titan remained imperturbable.

Dinners at Aunt Susan's house were legendary. They were relatively small—ten to a dozen people was the maximum capacity of the round table in her dining room—but the guests were selected for their appreciation of the good things in life and their talent for good conversation. The most novel of these dinners were the ones she gave for Morgan and a few of his cronies, because, except for the hostess, they were strictly male assemblages. Naturally, in my salad days I was not invited to any of her formal dinners, but she told me about them, knowing I had a yen for good food and fine wine, and she saved the empty bottles so I could add the labels to my collection.

During my college years on the New York University campus at University Heights (1901-1905) beer was the popular beverage. However, at class and fraternity dinners I was able to arrange for wine service. My frequent weekends at home also kept up my wine drinking habits. Another boon was the happy circumstance that my room-mate, Ten Eyck Reynolds, was an avid wine lover. We frequently went to New York for a spree to indulge in modestly priced bottles. The purse was lean in those years; the great wines were far too expensive. All in all, those college years and the summer vacations were by no means arid.

One episode is fixed in my memory. An investigation unearthed the fact that over two dozen graduate and undergraduate members of my fraternity (Psi Upsilon) lived in Yonkers. A few of us decided a dinner should be held to bring them into closer acquaintance, and I was delegated to make the arrangements. Knowing that support from the elder brethren would be essential to success, I consulted the local fountain head of Epicurism, Rufus King. He asked to see the proposed menu; approved it, but said: "What wines will be served?" To my mortification I realized that as most of the younger fellows were not wine drinkers, I had forgotten all about it. "My dear boy," said Rufus, "if we don't have wine, I cannot possibly attend. All that rich food would make me ill without wine to aid its digestion. If the price of the dinner has been fixed and the extra cost is a problem, I'll be glad to donate some bottles from my cellar." Which he did, to the gratification of all hands, for his wines were very good. They made the dinner a resounding success.

On my twenty-first birthday (January 9, 1905) I got a real break. Aunt Susan gave a dinner at her house in honor of the event. The guests were five college pals, my father and myself. I can still remember we ate oysters, terrapin, canvasback duck and venison. I wish I had kept a list of the wines and vintage years—they seemed marvelous. If memory serves, we had a fino Sherry before dinner, then Chablis, a Cote d'Or red Burgundy and Champagne for the birthday toasts. Coffee, Cognac and cigars rounded out the feast. Full to nearly overflowing, the six youths went off in a horse-drawn opera bus, to occupy a box in the theater

Father

Mother

The Youthful
Wine Lover

where a popular musical comedy was playing.

After my father's death in 1905, my mother, sister and I moved from the country to New York City. My brother Edward had passed away during my school years, and my brother Jack was still in the far West. Upon graduation from college in June, 1905 (age 21), I went to work in Wall Street as a "runner" for J. P. Morgan & Co. In those days, runners brought mail from the Post Office, carried messages to and from other financial establishments, delivered and received securities and bank checks and did endless odd jobs. One chore I always tried for was to take rare books and manuscripts from 23 Wall St. to the Morgan Library on 37th St. The librarian, Belle Greene, was a good friend of mine; she gave me a chance to rest my weary feet and chat with her about wine, women and song.

Belle Greene was a remarkable woman. By no means beautiful, or even good looking (her detractors called her ugly as a mud fence), she had irresistable charm and one of the best brains I have ever known. Unmarried, she had many ardent admirers. Her presence at social affairs was much in demand, but she rarely attended them; her career was the inspiration and joy of her life. Belle Greene became internationally famous as the criterion of the perfect librarian. Purveyors of priceless art and literature, hopeful of selling their wares to the great J. P. Morgan, knelt at her feet. At the start of this century, when very few women held posts of responsibility and discretion, her position was unique.

It was through Belle Greene that I met Isadora Duncan (for the first and last time). She was currently in New York with her troupe of dancers. A reception in honor of her visit to the city was held after the final curtain on the opening night. Belle asked me to attend the performance; but I was booked for the Opera, so she suggested I join her at the reception. This I did, resplendent in white tie and tails (most of the men wore dinner coats). I was duly presented to Isadora, who, in a diaphanous garment of some sort, was lying nonchalantly on a chaise longue, encircled by a group of admiring swains—they reminded me of a pack of hounds at bay with their tongues hanging out. The ballerina gave me a long, penetrating look, then moving her legs slightly to one side, invited me to sit on the chaise longue. She told me I reminded her of one of her former lovers of whom she had been very fond. I seemed to lose what little savoir faire I might have had at the age of twenty-three, and after a few inane regrets that I had not had the pleasure of seeing her dance, I kissed her hand and withdrew.

Next morning I had a telephone call from Belle. She was mad as a wet hen, said I had disgraced her and made a boob of myself. Later, she relented enough to say that she should have told me that when Isadora asked me to share the chaise longue, it meant I was to spend the rest of the night with her in something more than mere dalliance. Perhaps I missed the chance of a lifetime. The lady had a reputation of being proficient in other arts than the ballet.

My first honest dollars, earned as a runner, barely covered elevated railway fares and lunches. Down by the Battery waterfront, pushcarts sold clams (and oysters in season) for one cent each. I became a good customer—alas, no Chablis to go with them!

After a couple of years with J. P. Morgan & Co., spent mostly in cutting coupons from bonds that belonged to others, it dawned on me that old J. P. had no immediate plans to offer me a partnership, so if I wanted some action in Wall Street, bond selling was the best course. Stocks were considered to be only for gamblers or a means by which tycoons like Morgan gained voting control of corporations.

My sales trips often took me out of town, one of my ports of call being Scranton, Pennsylvania. I traveled on the Delaware, Lackawanna & Western Ry., which was called "The Road of Anthracite". In those days the steam locomotives were generally fired with bituminous coal, whereas the D. L. & W. used the much cleaner anthracite. A great fuss was made of this: placards depicting a fair young lady dressed in snowy white from head to foot proclaimed:

> "Here's Phoebe Snow, about to go
> On a railroad train to Buffalo.
> Her gown stays white from morn 'till night
> Upon the Road of Anthracite."

My father had been the consulting engineer in charge of the Scranton Waterworks construction, and a good friend of W. W. Scranton, the grandfather of his namesake, W. W. Scranton, Ex-Governor of Pennsylvania. I called on Mr. and Mrs. Scranton, and on each succeeding sales trip I dined at the Scrantons' in their huge house (with a well-stocked wine cellar), and grounds which covered an entire block.

On one occasion, just before leaving New York I received a note from Mrs. Scranton asking me to save a certain evening to dine with a number of other young people she wanted me to meet. Of course I accepted and, as usual packed my dinner suit, for I always wore it when dining with the Scrantons. I guess the dinner was a great success for most of the guests, about two dozen charming young ladies and gentlemen. For me, it was Waterloo, the worst social faux-pas of my life. Mr. Scranton and all the male guests were in tails, the ladies in ball gowns. One saucy debutante rubbed salt into my wounds—"I presume, Mr. Gould, that you New York society men think that we in the provinces have little knowledge of correct evening attire." All that I could say was "Touché".

Walter Lord, a biographer of note, wrote a book called *The Good Years,* which depicted life in New York and other eastern cities during the era from 1900 to World War I. Those years certainly were good to me. New York was an active arena where the socially-secure rich entertained in a style that will never be seen again, while the parvenus tried to gain recognition by even more lavish expenditure.

For young men of good repute but modest means, these festivities were a windfall. The debutantes of that period were closely chaperoned, so the stags could not entertain them in public places, even if they desired and could afford to do so. All contacts were at the young ladies' homes, at opera and theater parties, afternoon teas and private dances or large balls, such as the Junior Cotillion and Cinderella (a ball for sub-debs). The main requirements for a lad were a sound background, good manners, skill on the dance floor, punctuality in paying party calls, and possession of the proper attire. This consisted of a top hat, tails, cutaway coat and gloves. Canes and spats were swank but not obligatory. Unlike today, there were few places where this equipment could be rented; and as it was in fairly constant use, it was cheaper to buy it anyway.

When the season was over in New York, we took the show on the road. Newport, Southampton, Tuxedo Park, Bar Harbor and Saratoga Springs became Meccas. All this entertainment placed emphasis on wine and food of the first category, and I was lucky enough to be plunked right in the middle of it. At no other period of my life have I participated in such continuous rounds of good living and drunk so many bottles of wine of the best vintage years. My father's training helped immeasurably. When my hosts found that, in spite of my youth, I had a good knowledge of wine, they often asked my opinion of their cellars. Quite heady stuff for an impecunious youngster among tycoons!

FROM HOBBY TO CAREER

ALL GOOD THINGS come to an end. In 1906 I had enlisted in the ancient Seventh Regiment, N. Y. National Guard, and rose by slow stages from private to second lieutenant. Those service years were not without wine, for I found enough wine lovers in the ranks to stage company and regimental dinners featuring our favorite beverage. In June, 1916, the Seventh was ordered to Texas for Mexican border duty and stayed there until late November. Home-coming was a joyous event. We had fared badly both as to food and wine, and certainly made up for our lack.

But this was only a respite. War was declared in April, 1917. The regiment was mustered into Federal service in July and became the 107th U. S. Infantry Regiment 27th Division, with training headquarters at Spartenburg, South Carolina. There my ears played me false. The Division Surgeon General, after several tests, declared me unfit for overseas duty. It was a bitter blow not to go to France with the 107th, yet that may be why I am alive today, for my company (Co. I) suffered heavy losses.

World War I brought many young Americans in contact with wine for the first time in their lives, mostly without cost, for the French, in gratitude to their liberators, offered without stint bottles they had hidden from the Germans. (The Second World War was another opportunity and the subsequent long assignment of U. S. forces to European bases has done even more to interest Americans in wine.)

For me, there was some consolation for my sorrow over being left behind. Promoted to Captain, U. S. Army, I was given command of an infantry company at Fort Niagara, N. Y., near Niagara Falls and Buffalo. My military duties were nominal—the training of troops for guard duty at shipyards, arsenals and other plants producing matériel for the armed forces. My schedule gave me many free hours (two days at week-ends), which were well employed in wining and dining, for I had many hospitable friends in the Buffalo-Niagara Falls area who entertained me royally. Several were true amateurs of wine, maintaining fine cellars which I vigorously helped to deplete.

New York after World War I was a far different place than before. Entertainment was on a sober, simple scale. Wine importation had ceased in war years and bins were bare. Then Prohibition raised its ugly head; the bath-tub gin, speak-easy era commenced. Just prior to that catastrophe everybody but me bought all the authentic hard liquor available. I searched the small shops for wine bargains, finding a lot of good bottles at low prices because there was no demand for them. Very few people were interested in anything except booze.

Prohibition was a bitterly resented law which even those considered "law-abiding citizens" disregarded. Everyone had a bootlegger, or several, and patronized speak-easies. As well as the hooch, there was bootlegged wine, made generally from California table grapes legally shipped to New York and other eastern cities. Hijackers robbed bootleggers, revenue agents half-heartedly chased both, which brings to mind an amusing incident.

Down in Greenwich Village there was a little basement restaurant owned by a wine-loving Italian and his wife. They both became friends of mine. He made his own wine and also had a supply of sound Italian wines. He bought these from the pursers of ships when they docked in New York. One evening when I came in to dine and purchase wine, I saw at a nearby table three big, husky men who were not habitués of the place. My host informed me in low tones not to worry. The men were revenue agents all right, but they did not come to pinch him; they were his dinner guests who, at midnight, would escort him to a ship and back to see that he and his wines were protected from hijackers. Evidently they were wine lovers, for their rake-off came in bottles. I was asked to join the party and share in a celebration the ship's captain would stage. It was tempting, but I decided that returning home about 3 a.m. was too late for a working man.

After the war I went back to Wall Street and resumed my social activities, much less formal than in *The Good Years*. I married my first wife in 1924; we were divorced in 1928. (There were many marital problems in the speak-easy years). A few wealthy wine connoisseurs still had stray bottles in their cellars, but most bins were empty and replacements were hard to find. Except for Champagne, bootleggers found spirits far easier to dispose of and more profitable than wine. Home-made wine never became as popular as bath-tub gin. To keep up one's wine drinking, trips abroad were the best solution. Unfortunately, I had neither time nor money for such extended excursions, although once a friend who was driving to Quebec took me along as a paying guest. We dined and wined in grand style at the Chateau Frontenac for several days. The homeward journey was not so

The Gay Blade

The Sergeant

The Lieutenant

Camp Wadsworth, 1917

merry; we were searched by an inspector at the U. S. border, fined, and saw our half-dozen bottles of choice wine smashed before our very eyes. A sad sight.

The collapse of the stock market in 1929 found me tossing a coin to determine whether my accounts should be written in black ink or red. I left Wall Street in 1932, headed for a cyclone cellar; that cellar was in my Cousin Ray Winter's small house on River Street, Boston. I spent quite a bit of time putting it in order. Necessity forced me to find some form of gainful activity, but except for stocks and bonds there were few things in which I had experience. I toyed with the idea of giving dancing lessons or opening a contract bridge studio. Before a decision was reached, the repeal of Prohibition in 1933 offered a pleasing opportunity to turn a hobby into a vocation.

An old friend of mine, Grosvenor Nicholas, revived the dormant importing firm his grandfather had established in New York many years before. He was the sole U. S. distributor for a number of outstanding European houses, including Krug et Cie., Reims; Deinhard & Co., Koblenz; Hill, Thompson & Co., Edinburgh; Schroder & Schyler et Cie., Bordeaux, and Maraschino. Upon taking up the Boston agency for Nicholas & Co., I was able to make a modest living as a wine consultant and salesman; thus I could buy supplies at cost and restock our cellar in the River Street house. It is possible my cousin and I, with our friends, drank more wine and spirits than I sold.

The reputation of Bostonians for being good judges of wine is well established. In the 1930's most of the older families were still living in substantial houses with capacious cellars holding ample wine bins. Madeira was, and still is, a favorite of Boston connoisseurs. And Boston is the most likely place to find the few bottles of pre-phylloxera Madeira extant in the United States. It was a great pleasure to discuss, sell and write about wine in such an inspiring environment.

My association with distinguished amateurs and with fellow members of the wine trade is still vivid in my memory. Philip Dexter, Sohier Welch, Augustus Loring and others had fantastic cellars. The man of whom I was most fond was Charles R. Codman, a prince among men, with a distinguished military record in both world wars (aide to General Patton, W. W. II). He made annual visits to the leading European wine districts to taste the vintages and place orders for the old-line importing house of S. S. Pierce. A man of infinite charm, as well as a true epicure, he was beloved on both sides of the Atlantic. His wife, Theodora, was called by André Simon the Guardian Angel of the Boston branch of The Wine and Food Society, of which she was the Hon. Secretary.

From Boston I started a correspondence with Henry French Hollis that lasted many years. He was a former U. S. Senator who was commissioned by President Wilson to assist in French reparation projects after World War I. Liking France and liking wine, he stayed on in Paris to become acquainted with all the leading French vintners, and then developed an exporting business in wines and spirits. His judgment was greatly respected in wine circles. He shipped a lot of wine to me in Boston and my customers liked all of it.

In my files there is still a folder of his letters and price lists. In describing his offerings he used the most amazing terms—"gusty, gay, ripe, warm, elegant, subtile, honest, lively, flinty, exquisite, luscious, flowery, liquoreux, honey, lace, succulent, dulcet, baby's breath, pithy, rotund, fluent, violet, velvet, silky, meaty, cedar, mouse's ear, blackberry, raspberry, truffle, opulent, bees' wax, brittle, savory, toasted, suave, blunt, unctious, spirituel, musk, ethereal, gun powder". That's only half of them. What an imagination!

Senator Hollis had a fine cellar in the basement of the building in Paris where his apartment was located. One night in the 1940's a friend and I dined with him on what may have been the hottest night of the year; the temperature, I think, was 102°. Hollis had previously brought up from the cellar a Chateau Haut-Brion 1906, and a Richebourg, Domaine de la Romanée Conti, 1929. He and his third guest, a knowledgeable French wine merchant, debated on what to do about serving them. It was decided to run water from the cold faucet over the bottles. The water was not very cold, just cool enough to bring the wine to below room temperature. It was the first time I had seen this done, but the method worked well. To put these old red wines in the refrigerator or in an ice bucket might have been disastrous.

The year 1938 brought an end to importations from Europe and to the major part of my Boston wine business. Salesmen from California wineries had called on me frequently from 1934 onward. Their samples had little appeal. What seems to have happened was that during the long years of Prohibition many fine vines of the best wine grape varieties were uprooted so the land could be planted to other fruit crops. When Repeal came there was a rush to make wine from any grapes available (mainly table and raisin grapes) and ship it to eastern markets. To easterners used to the finer foreign vintages, these badly made young California wines were unacceptable. It took several years and the guidance of such knowledgeable wine merchants as Frank Schoonmaker to get the California wineries back on the right track. Perhaps Frank's greatest contribution was to put the name of each grape variety on the labels of the wineries he represented.

Another source of wine supply I investigated was the Finger Lakes wine region of New York State. Around 1830, vineyardists in New York and Ohio started to cultivate and improve the wild native grapes that grew everywhere. With development, these varieties of *Vitis Labrusca* began to yield useful wine of distinctive character (described as "foxy"). Their given names include Catawba, Delaware, Diana, Diamond, Dutchess, Elvira and Ives.

A distant relative of mine, Mrs. Waldo Hutchins, had a summer home, "The Chestnuts", at Bluff Point, N. Y. on Lake Keuka. My long visit with her in 1938 was all the more enjoyable because she liked wine and had a good cellar. Cousin Agnes and her daughter, Margaret, took delight in entertaining their friends, and thus I met many charming people, including one with whom I have kept haphazard but intimate contact for over thirty years. He is I. B. (Dick) Lucas of Markdale, Ontario. A lawyer (Q. C.) who seldom goes to his office, his chief aim in life is to teach people how to grow dwarf fruit trees in home gardens. On this crusade, Dick Lucas has roamed the face of the earth. His book, *The Footloose Gardener,* amusingly describes the journeys. During my stay at "The Chestnuts" I visited every prominent winery around Lakes Keuka and Canandaigua. The varietal wines at Widmer's Cellars, Naples, N. Y., took my fancy, especially the Delaware. I bought some of them.

A NEW LIFE UNFOLDS

SEEING no rosy future in Boston I went to California in 1940, my first visit to this Golden State, where in the Napa Valley I have put down new roots and now consider myself an Adopted Son. My headquarters was San Francisco—a focus from which visits can easily be made to the North Coast wine regions. Shortly after arrival, I received a telephone call from a total stranger. It proved a good omen, for the caller was Carl Bundschu, a man long associated with California wines (he would drink no other). Carl drove me everywhere, introducing me to vintners by extolling my wine knowledge, most of which he had to take on faith, for he had only just met me.

I made a few trips to the Los Angeles area. On one of these, Herman Wente and I were guests of the Los Angeles branch of The Wine and Food Society at a dinner featuring the introduction of Wente Bros. Pinot Chardonnay. There were many wine enthusiasts in the group—Phil Townsend Hanna, William Converse, Dr. Marcus Crahan and Harold Richardson in the forefront.

As California is a long state, it is hard to keep contact with its many wine areas from north to south. My interest has always centered on the North Coast Area, and visits to the southland are infrequent. This does not mean that there is less wine interest down there than in the north. There are several branches of The International Wine and Food Society in the south, while other groups hold frequent tastings and dinners. The large expansion in population is a potential asset for further progress.

Carl Bundschu had taken me to the Los Amigos Winery at Irvington (near Mission San Jose). I became interested in this small operation and its proprietor, Robert Mayock. Accordingly I returned to Boston for a few months, then shipped my few belongings (including about ten cases of French and German wines from the River Street cellar) to California and camped at Los Amigos to assist Rob Mayock. I picked grapes, helped in the crushing, fermenting, racking, filtering, topping tanks with new wine, making laboratory tests, bottling, corking and packing for shipment in wooden cases. Beaulieu and Los Amigos (the great and the small) were the only wineries I recall using wooden cases at that time. This was an all-around training course in wine-making, never to be forgotten. I also sold some of the wines through my San Francisco connections.

Living at Rancho Los Amigos was a fantastic affair, a five-ring circus. Rob Mayock (he preferred "Rob" to the more generally used "Bob") was the personification of Falstaff, except that he was not cowardly. Rotund, jovial, witty and somewhat boastful, he certainly was, with a store of anecdotes on a par with the Arabian Nights. His wife, Ann, a woman of intelligence and a marvelous cook, unselfishly let him have the center of the stage while she provided the background music. Their two sons, Douglas and Stoney, worked in the winery when not in school. Their daughter Sally, later a brilliant student at Mills College, was nearly her mother's equal in the kitchen. We had very little money, but we were all wine lovers and good trenchermen and lived in a jolly, carefree way.

My next move was to St. Helena at the request of Albert M. Ahern, who had recently purchased a small cellar from Charles Forni, a distinguished Napa Valley vineyardist. My job was to advise on the character and quality of the wines and to promote their sale. A lot of odd chores around the place came into the routine. The winery was called Freemark Abbey. This was too small an operation to cut much of a figure in the Napa Valley wine scene, and there was nothing I could do to improve the picture. I continued to give friendly advice, but took myself off the payroll. It is pleasing to note that after years of inactivity, the Freemark Abbey cellars were taken over in 1967 by a group of young men who have winemaking skills and own vineyards in Napa Valley. Their future looks rosy.

Then followed a couple of relatively idle years in St. Helena with trips to all the leading California wine areas. It gave me a chance to build up a cellar of the wines I liked best, plus the remaining foreign bottlings I had shipped out from the east. Little did I suspect that a turning point in my life was just around the corner, one that was to make me far happier than I had ever been before.

This was early in 1944 at a cottage colony called The Madrones, a mile or two north of St. Helena. The premises were owned and operated by Andrew Nemes, his wife and his sister. This Hungarian-American family were most considerate hosts. They kept the cottages neat as a pin and served excellent meals. In fact, they were much too generous with their guests, giving far more than the moderate monthly charges warranted. This preyed upon my conscience and I soon raised my own rent. Nemes was dumbfounded; nothing like that had happened to him before.

Shortly after I was installed in my cottage, Romilda Peri of Marysville, California, and Cavigliano, Switzerland, rented another one on the grounds. Being proficient in the Spanish language, she was aiding the agricultural project of importing Mexicans to work in the orchards and vineyards. (My war effort was confined to serving on the Ration Board.) We found we had many things in common, including a love of wine, and became fast friends.

Just how Romilda and I became acquainted is debatable. As I tell it, on the evening of her arrival at The Madrones, I sat in my pre-empted corner overlooking the rest of the dining room. As usual, I had a book beside me to read between courses and only vaguely noticed a female wearing jodhpurs, evidently a new guest. Seated by the front window of my cottage after dinner, I saw the same young lady strolling past my door, back and forth as on a picket line. After this had gone on for some time, I came out and said: "All right, I get the message; come in and have a drink." Romie claims she was innocently looking at some flowers near my cottage when I rushed out, grabbed her arm and dragged her inside, where with lustful leers I plied her with brandy. She escaped a fate worse than death by a hair's breadth. Both versions bear little semblance to the truth, but in conjunction they make a good conversation piece we use whenever we are asked how we met.

Romie went to Washington, D. C., early in 1945 to receive training for foreign service with the U. S. Department of War. She was sent to Beirut, Lebanon, that April, at which time we began a voluminous exchange of letters. In 1946 she resigned from her Beirut post, returning to her birthplace, Cavigliano,

Ticino, Switzerland, to live in the Peri family villa with her elder sister, Violante (dubbed by me "the Duchess"). I joined them there early in 1947.

The Duchess owned a small Chevrolet, but as rationing was still in force, gasoline was a problem. However, by hook or by crook, enough was accumulated to power an extended tour of the vineyards in Champagne, Burgundy and Bordeaux. The vintners, just recovering from the ravages of World War II, were busy restoring their export contacts, yet they found time to give us a warm welcome. Romie's knowledge of French came in handy.

As a rejuvenator, Ponce de Leon's fabled Fountain of Youth, even if he had found it, would be small potatoes in comparison with the *joie de vivre* of Romilda Peri and its contagious influence on all who know her. *La Petite Suissesse,* as M. F. K. Fisher calls her, is my ball of fire, a constant inspiration to the enjoyment of life. Small wonder our journey through France was a rollicking affair bringing never-ending surprises and delights.

There were so many high spots only three are here recorded. The first was the sight of an autographed photograph of Douglas MacArthur on the desk of Joseph Maurice Drouhin, when we visited his office in Beaune. The second was a simple supper at the home of Mme. Jacques Bollinger in Ay-Champagne. The repast was meager; the Bollinger 1934 and 1937, fresh from the cool cellar, were excellent. The charm of our hostess cannot be too highly praised. An aftermath to that pleasant visit occurred shortly after our return to Switzerland. Mme. Jacques had told us that in the strict rationing of food in France, rice was unobtainable (her favorite grain). There was no rice in Switzerland, either, but by driving down into Italy we found a supply and sent Mme. Bollinger all we could buy. No other present could have given her more pleasure.

The third episode was even more fantastic. It occurred at Reims. As I had been the Boston representative of Krug et Cie., a visit to the establishment was a must. The proprietors were busy when we called, so we were asked to come back before noon to sample some Champagne. Upon our return we were greeted with open arms; on the table were glasses and a magnum of Krug 1928! The year 1928 was a great one for all Champagne houses, and Krug was acclaimed the best of all.

So the story told to us, as we sipped this nectar, has an amusing twist. When the German occupation forces came to Reims, von Ribbentrop made his headquarters in that city. Before the war he had been a Champagne salesman. He knew the values of wine. Immediately he commanded that all the Krug 1928 on hand be sent to his headquarters. He was told: "Alas, all that vintage has gone! We will give you what later years we have." How then the magnum of 1928 we enjoyed in 1947? Well, the French are old hands at camouflage. The climax of our host's story was that after the war, upon receiving a plea from the King of England for two cases of Krug 1928 they gladly granted His Majesty's request.

In September of 1947, I sadly left the hospitality of the Peri sisters and went to Paris en route for Cherbourg (then the port of departure, as Le Havre was still bottled up with sunken ships). At my little hotel on the Left Bank, I found a message from the U. S. Lines, saying the sailing date would be delayed because of a dock strike. Ten days in Paris alone, not good at all except for a chance to wine and dine in high style. The Hotel Sevres-Vaneau served breakfast, but no other meals. However, the proprietor had a small kitchen and private dining room where his family had their meals. I became well acquainted with all of them and devised a way to crash the party by giving a farewell dinner on the eve of my departure.

There were eight of us in the small room. I did the marketing (the Bon Marché was just around the corner) and also bought the wines. I still have the handwritten menu: *Les Vins:* Vermouth Cinzano; Pinot Zessel 1942; Grand Vin Sec A. Lasserre, Bordeaux; Chateau Latour 1928; Chateau Ausone 1920; Blanc de Bergerac R. Guichard, St. Nexant; Champagne Heidsick Demi-Sec. *Le Diner:* Langouste Parisienne a la Grand Mode; Gigot de Mouton Pré Salé; Pommes de Terre Mousseline; Paté de Foie Gras Truffé; Salade de Laitue; Ile Flottante; Fruits; Café; Cognac. Some of the wines were strange to me. I found them here and there in small Left Bank wine shops. The langouste was a work of art. The largest in the market, it was boiled, taken from the shell, cut into small slices, then reassembled in the shell and highly decorated. A memorable bon voyage meal.

In June, 1948, Romilda sailed to New York and I went east to meet her. We were married there on June 23rd. It was a simple ceremony attended by a handful of my oldest friends, one of whom was Grosvenor Nicholas, who supplied our favorite Krug Champagne. After a brief visit with another dear friend, Rodney Jarvis, in the Berkshire Hills of Massachusetts, we returned by train to California and set up housekeeping in "La Casita", my old cottage at The Madrones. We lived there and in other rented houses until in 1961 we bought our present home at 1500 Wheeler Way, St. Helena.

My association with C. Mondavi & Sons began in 1949 and continues to be my main activity. Public Relations were then non-existent at Charles Krug Winery (and at most California wineries). I started a Visitors' Room and conducted tours of the

With Romilda in Greece

grounds and buildings, during which time I imparted as much wine information as the visitors could absorb. The Charles Krug Lawn Wine Tastings were my next project. The first issue of *Bottles and Bins* (the winery's quarterly publication) appeared in July, 1949. That and all subsequent numbers have been written by me.

My present schedule is very elastic. I have no office at the winery and no set working hours. Entertaining V. I. P.'s, attending wine tastings and writing all the sales literature are among my various jobs. When requested, I try to give constructive advice. It is on record that a few of my suggestions have been accepted.

This loose schedule provides ample opportunity for other pursuits along the wine trail. I am particularly happy over the part I took in starting the Napa Valley Wine Library. Many people believe the thought of having a wine library in Napa Valley originated with me. That is not the case. The idea was conceived by two people who were far too busy to organize the project, M. F. K. Fisher and James E. Beard. It was their brain child, but they laid the baby on my doorstep.

The first need was money. I begged my friends to help me. They responded generously. Other donations were made by the Bank of America and the Napa Valley Vintners. Major assistance came from the University of California, Davis, in the form of books and pamphlets sent us by Professor Maynard A. Amerine. The St. Helena Public Library gave us a home and has been a faithful ally. So, the Library came into existence in 1961. There was only one fly in the ointment, but a big one: nobody read the books. On the other hand, the annual wine tastings were so popular many people thought the Napa Valley Wine Library Association was a social society rather than a literary project, despite the purposes clearly defined in the By-Laws.

Now, the Library is on an even keel. The original Trustees have been succeeded by a complement of officers and a Board of Directors. There is good news about the books. They are being widely read, with some volumes on the waiting list. Another element of strength comes from the Wine Appreciation Courses, held several times a year under the supervision of Jim Beard. They are of great educational value. Meanwhile, the annual wine tastings continue to be heavily attended. All in all, there is now a good mix.

What of the future? I have a dream, perhaps just an old man's dream. Yet sometimes dreams come true. One day, our Napa Valley Wine Library should have a home of its own. The St. Helena Public Library has scant room for its own needs and cannot expand our space. What I hope for is a Wine Museum and Library. In addition to books, pamphlets, engravings and photographs there are valuable artifacts in Napa Valley which could be gathered together under one roof. There is ample precedent. Europe is full of wine museums. The Taylor Wine Co. has one at Hammonds Port, N. Y. and Fromm & Sichel is establishing one in San Francisco. Napa Valley, one of the world's leading wine areas, is an ideal place for a combined Museum and Library.

FOLLOWING THE WINE TRAIL

MY WINE PURSUITS in Europe take many forms, including research, visits to vineyards and wineries and dining at notable restaurants. Of these my favorite is La Pyramide at Vienne, thirty miles south of Lyon. Romie and I went there for the first time in 1947. We did not meet the proprietor, Chef Fernand Point, proclaimed the "great master" of all the cooks of France, because he was at the beginning of an illness from which he never recovered. We presented our card of introduction from Maurice Drouhin to Madame Point, who gave us a warm welcome. After a fantastic luncheon with numerous wines, I was shown the cellars, undoubtedly among the finest in France or anywhere else.

We have repeated our visits to La Pyramide whenever possible and have found that Fernand's widow, Madame Point, has maintained the excellence of the cuisine, which is given by Michelin 3 stars and 4 spoons and forks. Our last meal at Chez Point was on January 9, 1964, my 80th birthday, and thereby hangs a tale.

We were spending the winter months on the Italian Riviera when the question of where to celebrate my birthday arose. I said La Pyramide is the place I wish to be, and that ended the discussion. Accordingly, The Duchess, Romie and I set forth for Vienne by car with a couple of stop-overs along the way, including a visit and luncheon with Mark and Marcelle Chapoutier, whose wines are outstanding in the Cotes du Rhone. When we came to the Chapoutier office, after a few false turns, we saw an American flag over the door, an assurance we were at the right place. Somewhere along the line, I had become cursed with a malaise that made me feel lower than a snake's belly. After tasting a few wines I was put to bed at Chateau La Ciboise while the others enjoyed a delightful luncheon. All I had was a bowl of hot soup.

It was snowing hard when we arrived at the Residence, Madame Point's charming guest house where overnight visitors are lodged. A Saint Bernard dog would have been a welcome sight. Our rooms were large and well heated, so we dressed for the big event in comfort. Owing to the bad weather, there were only a handful of other diners, but the wines, food and service were impeccable. The Geneva office of Merrill Lynch had ordered a bottle of Champagne for us. Madame Point contributed a rich birthday cake with eight candles. All's well that ends well. I hope to feast again at La Pyramide, before the last trump, but never again in January—although Romie has already promised to take me there for my 90th!

There have been many more memorable wining and dining experiences. I spin these yarns when discussing wine with kindred souls, and am ready to do so with you, and you, and you. I have been to numerous repasts given by wine societies in various parts of the world. I attended all three of the Conventions to date of the International Wine & Food Society; alone at Chicago (1966), with Romie in Britain (1969), and in Paris (1971). The 1959 Convention of The Society of the Cincinnati in Paris was another opportunity for several days' association with rare vintages, and *la grande cuisine*. Thank God, the end is not yet.

In no other small community have we seen such a wealth of fine wining and dining spots as in Talloires (Lac d'Annecy) in the province of Savoy. The town has one 3-star, one 2-star and two 1-star restaurants. Romie and I went there to celebrate our fifth wedding anniversary. Where to stay was the first problem, for in June accommodations are extremely limited in that part of France. We made reservation at Le Cottage, arriving there the afternoon before the red-letter day, with time to unpack in our large suite overlooking the lake. Later we enjoyed the excellent table d'hote dinner.

That evening we met our host, Georges Bise, to discuss the next day's program. We told him we intended to have our celebration dinner at near-by Pere Bise, run by his cousin Francois Bise. "No! No!" cried he, "your dinner will be here. Pere Bise has 3 stars while Le Cottage has but 2, but we can give you as good, if not a better meal." So we three put our heads together to choose the food and wines, and our selection was:

The Wines

Fino Sherry (with
Hors d'oeuvres)
Champagne Blanc de Blanc
Henri Grevin 1947
La Romanée Conti 1927
Cognac
Fine Champagne

The Menu

Consomme froid en tasse
Ombles Chevallier braisés au Porto
Fricassée de vollaille Fleurs Alpes
Salade coeurs de laitues
Tous les fromages
Bombe Sibérienne sauce chocolat chaude
Friandises
Café

Next morning, without thinking of later meals, we ate a complete Continental breakfast in our room. Shortly after noon, we strolled over to Pere Bise for what we thought would be a light luncheon. We started out with an aperitif and then had:

Terrine Truffée au Foie Gras
Gratin de Homard Nantua
Carré de pré Salé au feu de Bois
Fromages de Savoie
Framboises Cardinal
Patisseries et Fruits

all this accompanied by Montrachet 1950. It was a substantial luncheon, which showed that the 3-star award was richly deserved.

I recall that the silent movies had a caption which appeared on the screen after a particularly tense scene: "Came the dawn". This would have been appropriate in our case, for it suddenly dawned upon us that we were surfeited with food and drink while we still faced a banquet that evening—and only a few hours away.

Stern measures were required. We requested Le Cottage to serve our dinner late. Then we drove to Annecy to a druggist for bicarbonate of soda. We spent part of the afternoon walking around the lake until we were ready to drop. Dead tired, we returned to our room: a shave for me and a bath and a short nap for each of us before dressing for the evening. We were pleased to find, however, that we had regained our appetite by that time! We felt more like gourmands than gourmets, but were able to do justice to a meal that proved the cuisine and the cellar of Le Cottage were indeed in the same class as Pere Bise.

But I shall put stars, spoons and forks behind me, for the nonce, and add a few more words about our life at home. No one who has visited the Napa Valley has left it without a longing to return. Romilda and I (neither of us born in California) have warm

With Romilda on Shipboard

spots in our hearts for every inch of this lovely place, and for the many charming people who have befriended us. Social life is carried on in an easy, informal style with no distinction between the wealthy and those with lesser worldly goods. Warm friendship develops without snobbery.

I like to think this congeniality among the inhabitants is fostered by the scenic beauty of the area—where every prospect pleases and man is not vile. The presence of wave on wave of cultivated vineyards, together with the wineries that turn the fruit of their vines into nectar fit for the gods, must have an ameliorating influence over all. How truly Robert Louis Stevenson expressed, in *The Silverado Squatters,* this lasting impress of Napa Valley wine when he wrote, "The smack of Californian earth shall linger on the palate of your grandson."

Yet, no matter how happy Romie and I are in St. Helena, there is, for us, a rival Shangri-La in Switzerland. In the little village of Cavigliano where Romie was born, she and "The Duchess" own a delightful stone house, "Casa San Michele", a part of which dates back to 1620. Several terraces running into the hillside have lawns and gardens, which provide outdoor living in good weather. Within, the small, cozy rooms (stone walls three feet thick) have an aura of olden days. My favorite part of the house is the underground cellar. There I keep precious bottles at ideal storage temperatures. Frequent trips to French, German, Swiss and Italian wine regions afford an opportunity to visit our vintner friends and to buy new wines for the cellar.

Yes, between St. Helena and Cavigliano, we get changes of scene, all associated with wine, that keep us out of the rut so easy to slip into when one stays overlong in one place, be it ever so pleasant.

THIS THING CALLED WINE

A LIFETIME of wine drinking and many years of research leave their mark on those who choose the Wine Trail as their favorite path. Thus, a little here, a little there, a personal philosophy of wine emerges. Like all others who indulge in these pursuits, I have one. Some will accept it, others reject it; to each his own. The great appeal of wine stems from its many contrasting aspects. What is right to Tweedledum may be wrong to Tweedledee. On one point, I think we should all agree. Wine could never have become a universally accepted beverage if it were as complicated as some wiseacres profess it to be. The self-claimed erudition of the wine snob is a grave menace to the novice who seeks enlightenment but is awed by pompous edicts, most of them mere hogwash.

This is not to imply that the more intricate facets of wine should be ignored completely. It is a question of personal desire. Those who are happy to drink wine, and to enjoy it without knowing why, are perhaps wise to let it go at that. But there are others who believe that the more one knows about the good things of life the more one appreciates them. To this latter group, in my estimation the simon-pure wine lovers, I heartily recommend diligent exploration of the inner sanctum. It will bring rich rewards. Here are some of the avenues to approach.

When opportunity affords, visit wine districts, inspect vineyards and wine cellars. Read the wine articles in newspapers and magazines (there are many more of them than you might think). See if your nearest public library contains any books on wine. If so, take them out to peruse at home. This may induce you to start a collection of your own. Attend wine tastings and lectures, asking questions on points that are not clearly understood. Above all, drink as many different types of wine from different wine regions as you can. Discuss their similarity or dissimilarity with others to get varying opinions, remembering that no two of us have exactly the same reactions to smell and taste.

Wine has been hallowed, through countless ages, by poets and sages. Like women and song, it appeals to the senses. Wine should be fun. Don't make wine drinking a drudgery that must be endured in order to keep up with the Joneses. Romance plays a leading part in the aesthetic enjoyment of wine. The time, the place and the girl, with soft background music, will make even an humble wine the nectar of the gods.

On many occasions I have been under wine's spell, and some written words in praise of wine are indelibly stamped in my memory. Such was the case when I first read a little book, *The Man Who Made Wine* by J .M. Scott (E. P. Dutton & Co., N. Y., 1954). This is not a technical work, as might be inferred from the title. It is a wine novel of the reminiscences of an old winemaker at a dinner in his honor, on the eve of his retirement after half a century of labor.

The book is steeped in romance throughout its 125 pages. At the ending of the feast, when all except the winemaker had left, a little boy approached, eating a large bunch of grapes. The old man lifted his glass to the child. "We who are on the way out salute you who are on the way in," he said softly. "There will always be good young wine coming on in the *chai* (wine shed) and good young fellows who love the vines. When you are a man, you will sit here and drink the blood of these grapes. May the good God show you what He has made me see."

Alfred Duff Cooper (Lord Norwich) completed his autobiography, *Old Men Forget,* shortly before his death in 1954. It contains an unforgettable tribute to wine: "On Sunday in London I could find nobody I knew. I went to dine alone at one of those station-hotels of clubs where in those days (1917) the food was simple and good and the wine cheap. Also it had a library. I ordered an imperial pint of Champagne, that admirable measure which, like so many good things, has disappeared from the world, and I took *Through the Looking Glass* to accompany me during dinner. I wrote in my diary the next day: 'As by enchantment, my melancholy left me and I knew that I should not be unhappy again. Courage came back to me which I had lost and I despised myself for having done so.' . . .. I should here, perhaps, acknowledge the consolation I have never failed to find in the fermented juice of the grape.

". . . Writing, in my sixty-fourth year, I can truthfully say that since I reached the age of discretion I have consistently drunk more than most people would say was good for me. Nor do I regret it. Wine has been to me a firm friend and a wise counsellor. Often, as on the occasion just related, wine has shown me matters in their true perspective, and has, as though by the touch of a magic wand, reduced great disasters to small inconveniences.

"Wine has lit up for me the pages of literature, and revealed in life romance lurking in the commonplace. Wine has made me bold but not foolish; has induced me to say silly things but not to do them. Under its influence words have often come too easily which had better not have been spoken, and letters have been written which had better not have been sent. But if such small indiscretions standing in the debit column of wine's account were added up, they would amount to nothing in comparison with the vast accumulation on the credit side."

Visitors to the Haraszthy Cellars, Buena Vista Winery, Sonoma, California, will find, painted on a cask's head, a tribute to wine that plucks one's heart strings:

"Back of this Wine is the Vintner
And back through the years his Skill,
And back of it all are the Vines in the Sun
And the Rain
And the Master's Will."

All wine lovers recall similar examples of the great appeal wine has to the mind and the heart. We should preserve and cherish them.

WINE IMMORTALS

MUCH HAS BEEN SAID and written about gradations in wine rankings. There is no common agreement; but a few simple distinctions can be made. *Vin ordinaire* (called commercial or standard wine in California) is, as the name implies, rather ordinary stuff. *Vin du pays* is the wine of a given district. It may be good or poor. The term "Regional Wine" is used to indicate the standard wine of a given area. When a district name is used, such as Margaux, Pauillac, Saint-Julien in Bordeaux, or Napa Valley, Sonoma, Santa Clara in California, the wine is apt to be of a better quality. The highest rating is given to wines produced and bottled by a specific proprietor—a Chateau or Domaine in France, a Schloss in Germany, a named winery in California, New York and Ohio. This is only part of the story, for wine ranking depends largely upon grape ranking. The aristocratic varieties like Chardonnay, Riesling, Cabernet Sauvignon and Pinot Noir will yield finer wines than their lesser brethren.

The truly great wines of the world are few and far between. Many experts believe they reached their zenith in the pre-phylloxera years (generally before 1870, although the blight struck some wine regions later on). I drank a few pre-phylloxera wines in the early 1900's. Unfortunately, I kept no record of them, recalling only they were marvelous. Undoubtedly, some of the post-phylloxera wines have been close to, if not quite on a par with, the fabled ancients. I recall beautiful Chateau bottled clarets of 1906, 1914, 1924, 1926, 1928, 1929 and 1934. The vintages of 1945, 1947 and 1949 were very fine. With German wines the year 1921 is generally considered the greatest of this century, and 1934, 1937 and 1949 only a step behind. In Champagne, 1928 was a sublime vintage, Krug's "London Market" Brut being predominant.

Those wines are gone forever, yet memory lingers. The days of yore will always be thought of as the "good old days". This is true from generation to generation. It depends on how young or old one is. Romance also plays a part. It is possible the wines of the past have been hallowed even beyond their undoubted worth. Facing the present we are, as the late Morton Shand so well explained it in *A Book of French Wines,* living in a new era of winemaking. It might be called the "quickie" way, because the time element is the chief difference between the old and the new. In a nutshell, while wine techniques are better than ever before and winery equipment is vastly improved, today's wines are not aged in wood or glass for as long a period as used to be considered essential. I leave to enologists the technical comparison of the new wines vs. the older ones. To me, the trend towards speeding up wine production has at least some disadvantages to the wine drinker. Present-day wines are, in the main, thinner than their predecessors, and they lack the full grape character. They are certainly not as long lived. For example, white Burgundies such as Montrachet, Meursault Perrieres and Corton-Charlemagne in the 1900-1920 era were expected to be good for ten to twelve years or longer. Nowadays, these and other white wines are apt to show signs of oxidation four years after their vintage date.

Be all that as it may, we must live with what we have, not with what we remember. Some very good wine is produced today. Improvement can be noted in certain wine regions, notably those of Northern California, Ohio and New York. While the whites and rosés may be drunk while young, the reds, Cabernet Sauvignon (the principal variety in Bordeaux) in particular, will improve with bottle aging. Storage is highly recommended when proper facilities exist.

The partnership of wine and food should always be considered. My advice is to drink as many great wines (from different countries) as you can, but only when the accompanying food is of equal quality. To serve a Romanée-Conti with a hot dog or a hamburger is not the proper caper. Even if one can afford it, it is not wise to drink great wine habitually, any more than one would eat caviar daily. Good sound wines and wholesome, well-cooked food should be the standard fare. One cardinal principle must be stressed; drink the wines of the area, wherever you may be. Every wine, great or small, tastes best on its native heath and when accompanied by the local food specialties.

When one has long been an octogenarian and is nearing nonagenarian rank, memories become a priceless asset. My philosophy of wine has been molded, to a large extent, by past experiences involving places, people and wine literature. I have duly recorded some of these episodes and the personalities associated with them. Now I wish to add a few more observations.

Probably the most valuable books on wine are technical works, some of the best written in French, German, Italian and Spanish. I have read several of the English language ones and profited thereby, but I am not an enologist and prefer non-technical books. In fact, I am more an amateur than a professional at heart. It was not my good fortune to know those great English wine savants, George Saintsbury, Charles and Francis Berry, Ian Campbell, Maurice Healy, Vyvyan Holland, A. J. A. Simons, Warner Allen, Raymond Postgate and Morton Shand. However, I know of them through their writings or have read about them in the works of others whose books are in my collection. The Napa Valley Wine Library, which I initiated, has a full representation of these and other outstanding wine authors. We also have the works of illustrious writers on food and wine, with Samuel Chamberlain and M. F. K. Fisher in the front rank.

The roll of those who have been my past associates in the enjoyment and promotion of our favorite beverage is far too long to enumerate here. Several have already been mentioned. Among others who linger in my memory of the California wine scene are Clarence Wetmore, Jerry Landfield, Idwal Jones, Harold Price, Edmond Rieder and Bill van Wyck (a boyhood chum from New York years). It would be unwise to name the living; there are so many, and omissions might be misunderstood.

In every branch of human endeavor, there are those who tower above all the rest; a few attain immortality. Of all wine celebrities, André L. Simon reigns supreme. Born in Paris in 1877, he died in London in 1970. During his life span of over ninety-three years, his dedication to the art of gracious living and his contributions toward a better appreciation of good wine and food have immortalized his name. Since his death, many tributes have been written, relating his long association with wine, his hundred-odd books and articles on the subject, the Wine and Food Society founded by him, and the many honors bestowed upon him by France, England and other countries.

Champagne with André Simon

Among the most personal of André Simon's many works are *By Request,* his autobiography published in 1957, and its sequel *In the Twilight* (his last book) published in 1969, when he was almost completely blind but mentally alert. Yet, despite the lure of André's writings, his spoken words showed, even more clearly, the mettle of this remarkable man.

What is dearest in my memory, and in Romie's, is the close personal friendship we had with him over many years. These include meetings in London, a visit at his home, Little Hedgecourt, East Grinsted, Sussex, England, and during the Wine and Food Conventions in Chicago and Great Britain. His remarkable knowledge of wine, his love for it and his charming way of extolling its virtues will never be forgotten. He was a friendly, warm-hearted man, the embodiment of all the qualities that make life worth the living. We shall not look upon his like again.

Now, for me, the pace of life must perforce be slowed. Still, I look forward to a few more good years of wine drinking in various parts of the world; and of talking and writing about it for the edification of younger travellers along the wine trail. To your health, dear younger sons and daughters of Bacchus!

"BOTTLES AND BINS" POTPOURRI

Wine Drinking — *July*, 1953

'TIS A PITY such a benign beverage as wine is, in the United States, a source of anguish as well as joy. We start off with the unpalatable fact that ours is not a wine drinking country. Hence wine is a stranger to most, and one is circumspect with strangers.

On the bright side, interest in wine is unquestionably increasing; particularly among younger men and women. Informative books in English are being added yearly to the many already printed in foreign tongues; national magazines are publishing wine articles with greater frequency; wine advertising is improving both in quality and quantity and our vintners are awakening to their responsibility for educating the public.

Where then is the anguish? Here's the way we see it. Americans are proud of their leadership in science, mechanical arts and production skills; and of their ability to do many other things better than the next fellow and to make more money. Contrariwise, Americans are rather ashamed of the undeniable national backwardness in the social arts and graces. They shrink from exposure to this lack of savoir-faire, and by thinking of wine in terms of sophistication, they are inclined to develop a phobia towards it.

Now, wine drinking may properly be classed among the social arts, but it is much more than that. Wine, a staple food in most countries, is consumed daily by many people of humble station who are a far cry from being social arbiters.

To bring the matter to a focus, everyone should keep in mind that a knowledge of wine is not a primary requisite to its enjoyment. True, the more anyone studies the subject, both from book and from bottle, the greater one's knowledge will be; and with greater knowledge will come higher appreciation, but that's just the post-graduate's degree.

Unfortunately, a few willful people foster the idea that they, and they alone, are wine authorities, and the sole keepers of the keys to the art of wine drinking. These self-crowned kings of Babylon have scared the everlasting daylights out of timid souls, who rather than risk mistakes reluctantly forego the pleasures of wine.

There is no such thing as a "wine authority". There are wine experts and amateurs of wine; but no authorities on wine drinking (wine making is another matter). You, only you, are the authority on what is, or is not, delectable to your palate.

That's all there is to it. Don't worry about making mistakes or showing ignorance. If you enjoy wine, go ahead and drink it, merrily cocking a snook at the egg-heads, the while.

The Subtle Alchemy — *January*, 1962

To find a term descriptive of good wine,
A word that captures all its qualities—
Its body, taste, bouquet, its mollities—
Demands a richer lexicon than mine.

How put in words that equilibrium
That comes from perfect practice of an art
Which Nature set within the sweet grape's heart
Before transplanting from Elysium.
So let pedestrian mortals such as we
Sit quietly and still the feeble tongue
While on the hillside, in their majesty,
The vine, the grape, the breathing leaf, unsung,
Perform for us their subtle alchemy
And bless the very earth from which they're sprung.

—Grace Bird

Wine and Elegance *October, 1956*

The world changes, and the people who inhabit it follow suit by altering their mode of living as one generation succeeds another. What was done in grandma's day is considered outdated and is discarded. The emphasis is now on simplification, labor saving and automation. Many of the changes are the offshoots of necessity. No matter how much we miss the "good old days", things ain't what they used to be, not only for the Old Grey Mare but for everyone. Common sense dictates we face facts and gear ourselves to the exigencies of today, lest ulcers take over. Granted. But can all this streamlining be carried too far? Yes.

Very few royal families still reign and court life, as practiced in its heyday, no longer exists. The so-called "Age of Elegance" is but a memory; yet while that era cannot be resurrected, and probably should not be in any case, some of the *mores* of those times can profitably be followed in the present day and age.

The Art of Gracious Living, molded of course to fit existing circumstances, is a priceless thing that should be ageless and ever desirable. Wine is, or should be, an integral part of that way of life. Therefore, let's use as much care in the selection of our wines for special occasions as is used in the selection and preparation of the food.

With family meals, good honest country wine may be just the trick. When the cuisine is exceptional, so should be the wine. We don't mean rare foreign vintages of necessity; many of our finer California wines are quite up to the job. The point is that fine food requires equally fine wine to savor it. Don't try to get by with the everyday jug.

Another word on this same theme. It is good for the morale to stage a memorable meal now and again. Bring out the finest table linen, the best silver, china and glasses. Decorate the table, light the candles. Then, with the delectable viands from the kitchen and our choicest bottles, the shades of the Knights and Ladies of yesteryear will again enter the banqueting hall.

Postscript to Eden

October, 1968

The Lord created Eden and
He knew that it was good,
And then he populated it
With man- and maiden-hood;
But Eve, seduced by apples, fell,
And Adam shared the flop —
When the Lord found out about it
He was mad enough to pop.

He called his toughest angels and
Commanded, "Boys, evict 'em!"

And then he sat upon a hill
To formulate this dictum:
"Since man degraded woman
And the wench did not demur,
I now ordain a Natural Law
To punish him and her."

"Hereafter, every living thing
Shall flower, conceive, decay;
It is the fitting evidence
Of my Eternal Way."
So beast and reptile, herb and tree,
And graceful trailing vine
Forthwith became obedient
Unto the Will Divine.

Thus Cain was born, dogs whelped, hens laid,
Sows farrowed in the field,
And corn and wheat and rye and oats
Began their annual yield;
Fruits ripened on the trees and then
Fell thudding to the ground,
Where mildew, rot, and insect pests
Fulfilled the ordained round.

But Cain, the child of sin, deplored
The surplusage of fruit;
"A waste," he thought (for he was more
Than just a murdering brute).
"I shall experiment," he mused

And after cerebration,
He filled a pot with windfall fruit,
And voila! — fermentation.

The luscious grapes, he learned, produced
The finest type of potion;
Full many a cup of it he quaffed —
And then he got a notion:
"I'll boil the excess fluid out
Of this—by Gad I will!"
So Cain was the progenitor
Of what we call the still.

The grape is still a noble source
Of beverage alcohol;
We've added other sources,
And in truth we love them all.
Eden is lost, but we'll concur
That since the world began,
The rise of spirits compensates
The graceless fall of man.

—Carlton A. Sheffield

Alice and Our Amateur — *January*, 1962

It was one of those glorious Indian Summer days that came later than usual this year to Napa Valley. In mid-afternoon, Our Amateur ambled into the winery grounds. He was hot and tired and knew just what to do about it—a quick trip to the Tasting Room was indicated.

After quaffing a glass, and then another, of cool Traminer (his favorite on a warm afternoon) he pondered on ways of prolonging his sojourn without wearing out his welcome. Deciding it couldn't be done, he graciously accepted still another glass and, with a sigh, took off.

Outside, O.A. came again into the bright sunshine—too bright by far, in his opinion. So he crossed the tracks and popped into the new building to locate a cool corner out of the path of visitors who were being guided through the cellars. Perched on a couple of full wine cartons—he likes wine both inside and outside his hide—he mused on the joys of living in Napa Valley and the goodness of life in general. He may even have nodded the while.

"Alice, where are you?" Our Amateur's head came up with a jerk. He looked about, or tried to, for nothing could be seen in the inky darkness. Again came the sepulchral voice—"Alice, where are you?" "What goes on here?" said O.A. "Who are you, and for that matter, who's Alice?"

"I am Lewis Carroll. I seek my little protégée, Alice." "Well, I'm a monkey's uncle or else I've lost my marbles," replied O.A. Then he recalled that a fellow named Carroll wrote a story about a girl named Alice, long ago. Could this be Wonderland?

"What the dickens can these birds be doing in Charles Krug Winery?" pondered O.A. "The kid ought to be drinking milk and leaving wine to her elders and betters. Carroll, I reckon, is old enough to have a snort. I'll offer him one, compliments of C. Mondavi & Sons, of course. Matter of fact, what with the shock and all that, I could do with more Traminer myself, if I can find a bottle. This building's strange to me; I don't know where the light switch is."

Just then, an eerie glow cast some slight illumination, enough to disclose a silver haired old man leading a very pretty young girl by the hand. "I have found Alice", said Lewis Carroll, "and now it's past my bedtime. I leave her with you. She is most intelligent, take care of her." With that he vanished. "Hey, you can't do this to me!" cried Our Amateur. "What in blazes am I going to do with a little girl? I ain't no bloomin' baby sitter." "Don't be impudent or my friends will fix you," piped Alice. "The Queen will say 'Off with his head,' and then where will you be?"

"So you got friends?" sneered O.A. "Where are they?" "Why all around you, can't you see them? There is the White Rabbit, and over there is the Frog Footman, Mock Turtle, Humpty Dumpty and the White Knight. The rest are around somewhere," retorted Alice.

"Wow!" yelped our old friend, "I must have taken a wee drop too much wine. I don't see any of these people—but," and he cocked an ear, "I can sure hear them. If that ain't corks popping out of bottles, I am the Jabberwock himself."

"Give me some of that Burgundy," called out Tweedledum. "Contrariwise, I'll drink it myself," from Tweedledee. Said the Walrus to the Carpenter: "This is elegant Chablis. We should have walked the oysters over here to go with it." "Glub, glub" came from another corner. "That's the March Hare and the Hatter," said Alice. "It's curiouser and curiouser." "Your darn tootin'," said O.A. "Tell the Cheshire Cat to stop grinning at me and to lay off the Traminer. That's the last bottle here and it's my private stock."

All over the place, bottles were being opened. Not being able to do anything about it, Our Amateur, always the philosopher, reflected that at least these queer people knew good wine when they found it. To voice his thoughts, Alice murmured: "Mr. Carroll told me Charles Krug Winery is the best in California. He wanted me to see it and promised to let me drink these wines when I grow up."

But by now Our Amateur was past hearing. He fell into fitful slumber wondering how to explain that he hadn't drunk all those bottles single handed. "Guess I'll just say I was in Wonderland, and Alice and her friends shot the works."

Harvest — *October,* 1960

What harvest brings the year?
Content, achievement, cheer,
Courage to face all ill,
Hope for good fortune still,
And strength to persevere.

What harvest brings the vine?
The benefice of wine—
Wine that gives joy and peace,
Blesses the year's increase,
And makes its toil benign.

—MIRIAM ALLEN DEFORD

The Wine Glass — *January,* 1962

OBJECTS made from glass have been found which are believed to date back to 2500 B. C. Just when goblets or other glass vessels were first used to hold wine seems uncertain; but since wine drinking is a social custom of great antiquity, it is reasonable to assume some of the early glassware was used for that purpose.

Whatever may have been the gradual adoption of glass as a

container for wine, the 17th Century A. D. was a boom period for the manufacture of wine glasses and goblets, reaching its zenith in Venice and in Bohemia. Many of the rarest and most beautiful specimens of glassware extant were created by Venetian and Bohemian craftsmen of that century. Unfortunately, most of these, undoubted works of art though they be, were highly colored or elaborately decorated. They have, therefore, far more value as *objets d'art* than as wine glasses.

The popular taste for colored glass was evident in the United States as late as the first decade of the 20th Century. Light red glasses for red wines and light green for white wines were considered *comme il faut*. In clear glass the height of elegance was attained by using cut glass. Wine glasses so cut were always heavy and frequently ugly, yet they did allow the color of the wine to be seen.

We believe it was not until after World War I that full recognition was given by Americans to the superiority of clear, thin unornamented wine glasses. These can now be found in various sizes and shapes; capacities range from about 4 oz. (for Sherry or Port) up to 10 oz. or over for great red vintages. The differences in styling will furnish the ideal glass for each well known wine type. They are modeled, more or less, from the traditional patterns of famous wine regions.

Ideas about the importance of matching a specific wine with a specific glass range from the sublime to the ridiculous. Purists insist a connoisseur's cellaret should contain sets of every well known style of wine glass. The no-nonsense school says "a wine is a wine is a wine" and it tastes the same whether drunk from the bottle, a glass, china mug or a paper cup.

Our suggestion is to start with an "all purpose" design holding around 9 oz. and made of relatively thin, clear glass. Fill about one-half full when serving. Then, add Rhine type glasses, with long stems; and, later, a set for Champagne. These are sufficient for all table wines. From there on, let your aestheticism and purse dictate.

While open-minded on the question of variety, there is one tenet regarding a wine glass on which we are adamant—how to hold it. All modern wine glasses have stems. The stem has an explicit function. It is the place to put one's fingers when the glass is raised (an exception is the habit of some wine experts of holding a glass by its base). The reason is obvious. When fingers are on the stem, the entire bowl of the glass is exposed to sight. The clarity and color of the wine is unmasked for visual pleasure.

We cannot understand why so many people, even some considered wine-wise, disregard the stem and place their hands around the bowl. Pictures of fashionable gatherings, balls, receptions and the like, show a gushing debutante with her glass clutched firmly around the top, talking to an Ivy League halfback whose hamlike mitt masks all sight of his glass, except, heaven help us, the stem.

Here is a challenge to wine lovers. By personal example and indoctrination of the younger generation, let's all try to show that the traditional and right way to hold a wine glass is by the stem. Hands off that bowl!

Noah and the Wine — *January,* 1968

When Noah bade the ark farewell,
And pensive sat to think a spell,
An unknown figure met his eyes,
Perchance a herald from the skies,

Who said, "Since you have done your best,
The gods will grant you one request."

"My dearest sir," good Noah said,
"The water here affects my head.
Because the sinners great or small
Were in it drowned, both one and all,
And so my wish will be, I think,
To have some other better drink."

His wish was granted in a trice,
The Vine was sent from Paradise,
With lessons how to make it grow,
And counsel good for him to know.
And Noah, filled with grateful mirth,
Bowed down delighted to the earth.

Then calling to his wife and child,
He told them both in accents mild,
What all the confab was about,
And quickly laid a vineyard out.
When five or six short years were o'er,
The bottles reached his second floor.

Against this you can nothing say,
He took his wine in pious way.
Like upright Dutchmen later born,
To the honor of Heaven he drained his horn,
And after the deluge it appears
He lived three hundred and fifty years.

So each of you can plainly see
That wine is good for you and me,
And also that a righteous man
Ne'er mixes water in his can.
Because the sinners great and small
Therein were drowned, both one and all.

Old Dutch song translated for the Holland Society by Miss Maude Fortescue

Speak Up

January, 1966

WHILE it does not appear in his published works, Mark Twain is credited with the remark, "Everybody talks about the weather but nobody does anything about it." Whatever its source, the quotation has become a byword. We are happy to leave the weather in the lap of Jupiter Pluvius (and the forecasters), but there are things in life all of us complain of yet few do anything to remedy, wine and food among them. Surely, these twin subjects should be of prime interest to readers of *Bottles and Bins.*

With both wine and food we are faced by two considerations: where to buy it and how to use it. Concerning wine the problem is to locate reliable sources of supply and to devise means for adequate storage. The latter is a personal task often calling for great ingenuity, the former may require a Treasure Hunt to find dealers who truly know their trade.

English and American wine devotees of the old school have fond recollections of contacts with Wine Merchants. Members of an honored profession, these purveyors of distinguished bottles were not merely sellers of wine. They were advisors to their customers, and became guide, counselor and friend to all who crossed their thresholds. The proprietor and his assistants were able to explain their wines and learn the requirements of each patron to thus ensure the best value for money spent. Another service was the storage of a client's wine, if home cellars were lacking.

Are Wine Merchant Days gone? To a large extent, yes, because those men made a life-long study of wine, were themselves wine connoisseurs and enjoyed educating others. Very few present-day sellers of wine have such qualifications. Could Wine Merchant Days be resurrected? Again, the answer is yes, but it will take a lot of doing, by the people who buy and drink wine. We must express ourselves forcefully.

Wine drinkers should tour wine shops just as they tour wineries. Inspect the inventory and see how it is displayed. Discuss wines with the proprietor and the staff. Pay particular attention as to how the wines are stored. If fine wines are stood upright on shelves under bright light, suggest they might be better treated. Expound the value of racks where bottles can lie on their sides without exposure to light and heat. Advise keeping the main supply of the rarer wines in their original cases under proper storage conditions. In short, if the dealer lacks knowledge tactfully educate him on how best to select, store and explain his wines—but don't be pragmatic about it. Intelligent retailers will respond kindly to this treatment. If yours turns a deaf ear, find a better one. Should all of us follow this course, the delinquents would fall into line; some might even revive the old custom of storing a patron's wine, (due to lack of space, a fee might be required).

Another way to express ourselves occurs when we dine out. Examine the menu and wine card with care. The art of ordering a meal is the hallmark of a gourmet. Discuss the food and the wines with the Maitre d'Hotel and your waiter. This will create the impression that you are particular about what you put into your belly and expect well prepared and properly served food and expert wine service. If a dish is not what it should be, send it back, explaining why it is not satisfactory. If a wine is not in good condition, do likewise. But when a dish is particularly pleasing and a wine of exceptional merit, praise them. There must be compliments as well as complaints.

Millions of dollars are spent to ascertain the public demand. If people who have money to spend on wine and food verbally indicate what they want—and what they won't accept—merchants will follow their wishes. In wine buying, when you can't find your favorites in a shop, ask the proprietor to order them for you.

If a restaurant does not list the wines you prefer, suggest they may be added to the wine card. Many readers of *Bottles and Bins* have taken such action to their own satisfaction and to the benefit of Charles Krug wines. A consumer's recommendation is the most effective kind of advertising. Speak up!

Wine Grapes *January,* 1965

The grapes are like rare jewels
Hanging in clusters on their vine.
Green, gold and purple too
Have grown so,
Even before man measured time.

The wine that comes from each of them,
Whether palest pale or ruby red,
Makes the simplest meal a feast

And even burdened hearts feel glad.

As Jesus once a miracle wrought,
And for the wedding guests
Changed water into wine;
You too can give, with friendship blest
This wealth of nature so sublime.

—JEANNE VOLLMER

Setting the Stage *October, 1958*

IN COUNTRIES where wine is considered an essential part of the the daily ration, its consumption at the dining table is taken for granted, and no artifice nor maneuver is required to call attention to it. Receptivity is present, yes, and anticipation too. If not offered wine, the diners call for the bottles of their choice or demand the wine list.

Lacking this atmosphere of friendly expectation in the United States, wine has a far harder row to hoe. Those of us who believe the world would be a better place if more people drank wine, and who try to make this beatific doctrine more widely accepted in our native land, must resort to the power of suggestion to promote a larger national consumption. We must set the stage.

Dining at home presents no problem. Host and hostess give full play to their gastronomic talents, and serve forth the treasures from their cellars. No small part of the sensory pleasure of a memorable meal comes from a well appointed table. Mid candle light and floral decoration, the finest linen, ancestral silver, the choicest china, and the clearest crystal make their bows.

Transport the scene from one country to another, from city to city or to any suburban estate and the general picture remains the same, in spite of differences in language and in local cuisine and wines. Whatever the culinary scheme may be, wine glasses will always have their traditional place in the drama.

Public dining is another matter. In the United States one does not find the wine-mindedness that prevails in Europe. We don't refer to snack bars and the like. Wine and the hasty meal are incompatible. The comparison is between American hotels and restaurants which stock wines and their foreign counterparts.

True, most of our establishments holding wine licenses also have a wine list (seldom shown unless requested), or make reference to wine on the menu; but the expectation that wine will be ordered seems lacking. Few waiters or waitresses will mention it; fewer still will have intelligent suggestions as to appropriate selections.

Bottles and Bins has harped on this for years. Fortunately, much is being done to combat the apathy of our bonifaces, and quite a number of proprietors now realize wine education is a required course for the server as well as for the consumer if we are to become a nation of wine drinkers. We suggest the use of a not so secret weapon that might be as potent as David's little slingshot.

What does one see in a public dining room in Europe that is conspicuous by its absence in the American hotel or restaurant? A wine glass! On both continents the room will contain tables and chairs and a buffet or sideboard. There will be linen, china, silver, salt and pepper containers and water glasses, but, with us, no wine glasses.

Just as tableware suggests food will be eaten, wine glasses suggest wine will be drunk. They are an eloquent reminder of the gastronomic affinity of food and wine. If not required, they may be subsequently removed, but they should be "on stage" when the curtain goes up.

Calling all managements! When your tables are set for expected guests, remember that first impressions are apt to be lasting ones. Attention to the niceties of table setting, floral display and lighting will favorably impress your patrons. And, for Epicurus' sake, don't forget those wine glasses. They are the vital link from cellar and bottle to palate.

The Fisherman's Feast — *April,* 1971

Of all the gracious gifts of Spring,
  Is there another can surpass
This delicate, voluptuous thing, —
  This dapplegreen, plump-shouldered bass?
Upon a damask napkin laid,
  With exhalations superfine
Our gustatory nerves pervade,
  Provoking quenchless thirsts for wine!

The ancients loved this noble fish;
  And, coming from the kitchen fire
All piping hot upon a dish,
  What raptures did he not inspire?
"Fish should swim twice," they used to say,—
  Once in their native, vapid brine,
And then again, a better way—
  You understand; fetch on the wine!

Ah, dainty monarch of the flood,
  How often have I cast for you,

How often sadly seen you scud
  Where weeds and water-lilies grew!
How often have you filched my bait,
  How often snapped my treacherous line!
Yet here I have you on this plate, —
  You shall *swim* twice, and *now* in *wine*.

And harkee, garcon! let the blood
  Of cobwebbed years be spilled for him, —
Ay, in a rich Burgundian flood
  This piscatorial pride should swim;
So, were he living, he would say
  He gladly died for me and mine,
And, as it were his native spray
  He'd lash the sauce—what, ho the wine!

I would it were ordained for me
  To share your fate, O finny friend
I surely were not loath to be
  Reserved for such a noble end;
For when old Chronos, gaunt and grim,
  At last reels in his ruthless line,
What were my ecstacy to swim
  In wine, in wine, in glorious wine!

Well, here's a health to you, sweet Spring
  And prithee, whilst I stick to earth,
Come hither every year and bring
  The boons provocative of mirth;
And should your stock of bass run low,

However much I may repine,
I think I might survive the blow,
If plied with wine and still more wine!

(*Eugene Field "Second Book of Verses,"* *Scribner* 1893)

Wine Traditions *April*, 1963

AMONG the brightest facets of wine enjoyment are the many traditions that have been handed down through the ages. Here are two that recently came our way.

A charming Swedish lady told us her son knew the ritual of the toast Skoal (Skol). He sent us this memorandum.

"Drinking habits in Sweden are probably more complex than in any other country. It would be quite impossible to explain all the rules on this small slip of paper.

"One thing, however, must always be remembered. When sitting down for a meal you are not allowed to drink except if someone else wants to drink. At least two glasses must be raised at the same time.

"If you want to drink you grasp your glass staring at the person with whom you intend to drink. Both persons raise their glasses, they drink, after which the glasses are held at the level of the third waistcoat button. You stare into the eyes of your opponent, bowing slightly (hardly noticeable). The glasses are then placed on the table. Within three minutes your opponent should answer the toast (skol) in the same way. A guest is not allowed to toast the hostess. This procedure particularly applies to wine drinking.

"When consuming 'snapps' (usually taken with the first course) all those around the table raise their glasses at the same time, and the drinking is done in the same way as previously described. This, however, takes more time as you must stare everybody into their eyes before emptying your glass. A snapps-glass should be drained in one gulp. Refusal to do so is considered a sign of extreme weakness usually found among non-Scandinavians. This kind of toast is always proposed by the host."

A reader of *Bottles and Bins,* Major Bernard Graf Elfert, sent us a Christmas greeting and told us of a family tradition which impressed us so much we wish to share it.

"At Christmas time each year there are usually articles in the press concerning the various customs and observances connected with the Christmas season. My family has a very old tradition which, because it is a custom which deals with wine, may prove of interest to you. It is the custom of the Christmas Wine. I do not know the origin of the custom itself, but we have observed the tradition for generations. We are descendants of the house of D'Elvert of Vianden, Luxembourg, and that may be whence the custom came. This is the tradition:

"A silver tray is set before the chief of the family with a silver ewer and goblet upon it. The ewer is partly filled with wine (this is the wine of Christmas Present), and beside it sits a small flask (we use a little stone bottle that is very old) which contains the wine of Christmas Past. This is usually performed after the blessing and just before the Christmas dinner. The wine of Christmas Past is opened with the words: 'We open the wine of Christmas Past and bring to our table the spirit of our yesteryears.' Then the wine of Christmas Past is added to the wine of Christmas Present with the words: 'As we are, so is this wine of the present, from the past and journeying to the future.' The members present then pass their glasses to be filled and the chief pours the first wine into the goblet and then fills the other glasses. A toast is then made according to this formula: 'May the spirit of the Christ Mass fill our hearts and abide in them now and through the New Year to come. We share this wine with all our house and pray that they may, in spirit, be with us. God bless this house and bring us peace.' So saying the chief touches his glass to the goblet (poured for those not present at the table), and then the glasses are touched around the table and the toast is drunk. The wine in the goblet is put into the flask and will next season be the wine of Christmas Past.

"The custom seems a significant tradition and in times like these there are perhaps too few such ties with our past that are not being swiftly cut. There seems to be no rule as to the type of wine but it must be sufficiently sweet that it will not go bad through the year. This is one of the traditions of my house that I have always found very impressive and beautiful. Perhaps you may also find it of interest."

The Origin of Wine — *January*, 1966

Some caveman—or, more like, his wife,
Trying each wild fruit and berry,
Surely one day discovered grapes
Were sweet and wholesome — very.
So they plucked all that they could tote,
And more than they could eat —
Then found the residue, when squeezed,
Made a delicious treat!
Thus from that humble accident
Arose the drink divine

That we, their far-off progeny,
Enjoy today as wine!

—Miriam Allen deFord

Seasonal Fantasia

January, 1954

THE OTHER NIGHT we were (metaphorically) strolling through a Napa Valley vineyard. The recently pruned vines were just dark stumps, save for a few that still wore the tattered remnants of their multi-colored autumnal finery.

'Twas two o'clock in the morning with only a moon, just past its full, for illumination. No one was in sight, so we sat on an old grape box to enjoy the solitude. A night for meditation, if ever there was one.

Our thoughts drifted back to what Napa Valley may have been in the early years of its vines, the years of Charles Krug and the hospitality of Krug Ranch. Then we roamed still further backward to the Spanish era, to the days of Junipero Serra and the wines, crops and herds of the Missions.

Distances are as nothing in dreams and reveries, so we sped across the continent to the Revolution and before that to Colonial Days. Indubitably, in the times of Washington, Franklin, Jefferson, and their contemporaries, our forefathers knew and practiced a way of living far richer and fuller than most of us have today.

Then we started to think of present times, but were diverted by the appearance of a solitary figure which, upon closer approach proved to be Our Amateur, obviously hiding something under his coat.

After exchanging greetings, he sat down beside us. We asked him what he had inside the coat, suggesting it might be a kitten he was about to drown in the Napa River. O.A. let out a lusty guffaw, and said: "Some kitty, all right, but from the river, not going there. I put it in a couple of hours ago to cool off," Whereupon he produced a slightly moist bottle of Krug Traminer and we gave "kitty" a chance to purr in our throats.

When asked what he thought about the world, Our Amateur replied: "Things are bad. When I was a boy I used to believe the world was a big place, lots of different people. Then Wendell Willkie spoke of 'One World'. Now everybody talks about two worlds—Free and Iron Curtain. Heck, no matter what way you slice it, it still comes out a Bologna of wars, hot, cold and warmed over; of strikes, sit-down, stand-up and squat; of nose thumbing, name calling and general cussedness. Yep, it's a mess."

We sat in silence for a while, passing the Traminer back and forth. Pretty soon the moon got brighter, and the night mellower. We agreed that, after all, there is still one season of the year when the Free World, at least, brings forth its best. The best from the heart, the larder and the cellar. Friendliness, good will toward man, feasting and merrymaking prevail. Thank God this can still be so.

After a last, lingering "discussion" of the bottle, we wished each other a Merry Christmas and Happy New Year and went our respective ways.—Gentle Reader, we wish the same to you!

Year's-End Dyad

January, 1957

"God rest, God rest ye merry, Gentlemen,"
The carols fade away across the lea.
The Holy, Blessed Child is born again
To save a world for all humanity.

Sweetly the chimes ring out upon the night,
And as the choristers commence to sing,
Is born to every man for his delight
Israel's Saviour, Israel's Baby-King.
Let us fill all glasses, every one,
This is indeed a time to pour the wine
To drink a toast to Heaven's only Son
Born in a stable 'midst the lowing kine.
Fill up the glass till it glows ruby bright.
Sing praises to the Lord this Christ's Mass Night!

The welkin is ringing as we drink tonight.
Raise, raise your merry voices heaven-high.
The happy stars are shining golden bright,
Although another year is about to die.
The punch-bowl is filled with mellow burgundy,
Mulled and well spiced and passing good withal.
The glasses shine that wait for you and me
And all the guests assembled in the hall.
Although the Old Year is about to fly,
There'll be no moaning at the fellow's bier;
For we are feeling merry, you and I.
Eagerly we await another year.
What will it hold for us? An argosy
Of happiness and merriment and joy?
What will it hold for you, and what—for me?
Here he comes now—he seems a sturdy boy.
Give him a glass, he too must have a glass
With all of us to watch the old year pass.

—William van Wyck